11/07

Behind the Museum Door

Poems to Celebrate
the Wonders of Museums

selected by Lee Bennett Hopkins   illustrated by Stacey Dressen-McQueen

Abrams Books for Young Readers, New York

Artist's Note

Acrylic paint, oil pastel, and colored pencils were used to make the pictures for *Behind the Museum Door*. My inspiration was drawn from remembering the thrill of a school field trip. It was exciting to discover ways to translate the wonder of all those subjects I learned about into pictures.
—SDM

Library of Congress Cataloging-in-Publication Data:
Hopkins, Lee Bennett.
Behind the museum door : poems to celebrate the wonders of museums/
selected by Lee Bennett Hopkins ; illustrated by Stacey Dressen-McQueen.
p. cm.
ISBN 13: 978-0-8109-1204-5
ISBN 10: 0-8109-1204-X
1. Children's poetry, American. 2. Art—Juvenile poetry.
I. Dressen-McQueen, Stacey, ill. II. Title.
PS3558.O63544B445 2007
811'.54—dc22
2006013576

Book design by Vivian Cheng
Production manager: Alexis Mentor

Printed and bound in China
10 9 8 7 6 5 4 3 2 1

HNA ■■■■■
harry n. abrams, inc.
a subsidiary of La Martinière Groupe
115 West 18th Street
New York, NY 10011
www.hnabooks.com

To Elizabeth Harding—
who opens doors
—LBH

To Rob, Finn, and Emma with
love; and to Carol and Lyle
Dressen for everything, always
—SDM

Behind the
Museum Door

by Lee Bennett Hopkins

What's behind the museum door?

Ancient necklaces,
A fur of mail,
Armor of knights,
A peasant cart,

Bronze wagons,
Vintage cars,
A planetarium,

high-ceilinged,
halls,

with stairs

Priceless old coins,
A king's golden throne,
Mummies wrapped in linen,

And,
Yes
A dinosaur bone.

Suit of Armor
by Beverly McLoughland

In its human shape
Of molded steel,
It looks as though
There's someone real

Inside. You knock:
"Hello in there,"
And hear a dull
Echo of air

As though a voice
Were drifting through
The lonely centuries
To you.

Mummy

by *Myra Cohn Livingston*

So small a thing
This mummy lies,
Closed in death
Red-lidded eyes,
While, underneath
The swaddled clothes,
Brown arms, brown legs
Lie tight enclosed.
What miracle
If he could tell
Of other years
He knew so well;
What wonderment
To speak to me
The riddle of
His history.

To the Skeleton of a Dinosaur in the Museum

by Lilian Moore

Hey there, Brontosaurus!
You were here so long before us
Your deeds can never bore us.
How were the good old days?

Did you really like to graze?
Did you often munch
With a prehistoric crunch
On a giant tree—or two—or three
For lunch?

As you went yon and hither
Were you ever in a dither
When your head and distant tail
Went different ways?

Did you shake the earth like thunder
With your roars and groans?
I wonder. . . . Say it's hard
To have a conversation
With your bones.

Wheels
by Jane Yolen

What about that first man
standing in Mesopotamia,
circles in his eyes
from staring at the sun.
What about that first woman
sitting in Mesopotamia,
considering spinning,
inventing the hub.
What about those children
playing in Mesopotamia,
making reed whistles
and rolling hill hoops.
It could have happened that way,
it could have started
with the sun,
                the thread,
                        the whirling toy
until the plains of the world,
until the mountains,
until the valleys and the seashores
were crisscrossed
with straight lines of roads
to bear the burden
of all those wheels.

Museum Field Trip

by J. Patrick Lewis

A stand of stone
Makes its debut—
Now better known
As David II.

We took this trip
To watch them knock
A handsome chip
Off your old block.

I shout, *Rock on!*
The crowds increase.
You're such a con-
Versation piece

That viewers snake
In endless queue
And never take
Their eyes off you.

Museum

by Felice Holman

Pictures on the wall
look into lives
back when
I was not
anyone at all.
They smile
frown
play chess
walk to town
pat heads
of children
see them
to their beds.
They seem so real
and near
but they are fixed there
on the wall
and I am
here.

Stirring Art
by Heidi Bee Roemer

Beauty
suspended in
suspense.

A breath of air
awakens
lifeless form—

See
it
dance.

Clay

by Marilyn Singer

It all goes back to clay

Beads and bowls and bricks
   baked and built into houses
Pots and paints and possibly poetry
   scratched on terrene tablets
   all those many years ago
Jars to hold cool water
Jars to hold dry bones
A legend of lives lived
   plain or fancy
   foolishly or well
A history of the world
   in this earth unearthed

It all goes back to clay

Journey of the Woolly Mammoth

by *Maria Fleming*

On pillared legs, with tread of thunder,
you trudged across the endless tundra,
a mountain of fur, twin tusks thrust high,
back hunched beneath the weight of the sky.

Until you met some unknown doom,
disappeared into an icy tomb,
a secret buried underground,
ten thousand years lost...

Then found.

You walk again inside these walls,
a ghost that haunts museum halls.
Ice Age icon, here enshrined,
once frozen in earth,
now frozen in time.

O Trilobite

by Alice Schertle

O trilobite, there are a few,
here in the Fossil Room, of you.
Once billions strong you ruled the sea,
a Cambrian Age majority.
O trilobite, when life was new,
an upstart, just a cell or two,
experimenting, rearranging,
tinkering and always changing,
you were a breakthrough in design.
Life tried you on. The fit was fine.
An exoskeleton for skin—
a shell without, no bones within—
a pointy tail of modest size,
some jointed limbs, and compound eyes
that look around in each direction
simultaneously. Perfection!
You swam above the ocean floor.
Life made a billion billion more.
You were the model that was right
for Cambrian times.
O trilobite.

The Moccasins
by Kristine O'Connell George

A pair of tiny moccasins
standing in a neat straight line,
standing quietly behind glass.
On display, a child's small shoes,
buffalo hide, beaten soft,
faded brown, a whisper of dust.

Once, one fell off when she ran,
she tucked them under her arm
when she waded in the stream.
She curled her toes up inside
when she crouched to see what was
inside a ground squirrel's hole.

Watch for her tonight—tiptoe—
across the cold tile—open—
the glass display case—reclaim
her shoes. Watch for her tonight,
running, running soundlessly
into the moonlight, leaving
no footprints.

Tales in Tapestry

by Sandra Gilbert Brüg

Tales of chivalry, cruelty, battles, bloodshed,
victory—heroes, heroines, kings
their fearsome deeds depicted
in exquisite woven scenes.

Whose fingers held the bobbins?
Whose hands these fibers wed?
Or was it spiders, traced designs this fine
with silk and golden thread.

Sumptuous panels, huge ... *immense*,
costly made for grand display;
centuries old—yet bold enough
to capture hearts today.

Gaze long and deep at tapestries;
intensely human folk you'll see
and by their kinship you can touch
the stream of all humanity.

Away Away—I bid you go
to feast upon the lasting glow
of fascinating tales that show
other lives in other times—

inside museum doors.

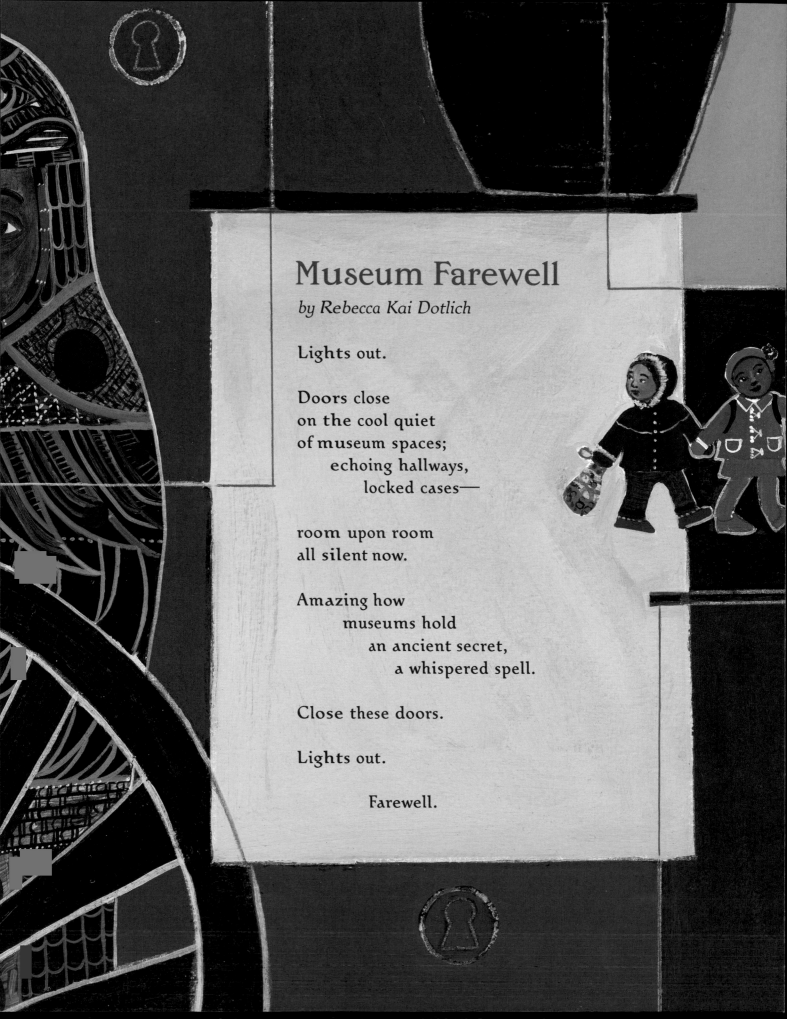

Museum Farewell

by Rebecca Kai Dotlich

Lights out.

Doors close
on the cool quiet
of museum spaces;
    echoing hallways,
        locked cases—

room upon room
all silent now.

Amazing how
    museums hold
        an ancient secret,
            a whispered spell.

Close these doors.

Lights out.

    Farewell.

ACKNOWLEDGMENTS

For works used in this collection, thanks are due to:

Sandra Gilbert Brüg for "Tales in Tapestry." Used by permission of the author, who controls all rights.

Curtis Brown, Ltd., for "Museum Farewell," by Rebecca Kai Dotlich. Copyright © 2007 by Rebecca Kai Dotlich; "Behind the Museum Door," by Lee Bennett Hopkins. Copyright © 1973, 1995 by Lee Bennett Hopkins; "Wheels," by Jane Yolen. Copyright © 1995 by Jane Yolen. First appeared in *Cricket*, published by Carus Publishing Group. All reprinted by permission of Curtis Brown, Ltd.

Maria Fleming for "Journey of the Woolly Mammoth." Used by permission of the author, who controls all rights.

Kristine O'Connell George for "The Moccasins." Used by permission of the author, who controls all rights.

Felice Holman for "Museum." Used by permission of the author, who controls all rights.

J. Patrick Lewis for "Museum Field Trip." Used by permission of the author, who controls all rights.

Beverly McLoughland for "Suit of Armor." Used by permission of the author, who controls all rights.

Marian Reiner for "Mummy," from *The Way Things Are and Other Poems*, by Myra Cohn Livingston. Copyright © 1974 by Myra Cohn Livingston; "To the Skeleton of a Dinosaur in the Museum," by Lilian Moore. Both used by permission of Marian Reiner.

Heidi Bee Roemer for "Stirring Art." Used by permission of the author, who controls all rights.

Alice Schertle for "O Trilobite." Used by permission of the author, who controls all rights.

Marilyn Singer for "Clay." Used by permission of the author, who controls all rights.